1000

Handmade Greetings

creative cards and
clever correspondence

QUARRY

First published in the United States of America by
Quarry Books, a member of
Quayside Publishing Group
100 Cummings Center
Suite 406-L
Beverly, Massachusetts 01915-6101
Telephone: (978) 282-9590
Fax: (978) 283-2742
www.quarrybooks.com

Library of Congress Cataloging-in-Publication Data

McFadden, Laura.
  1000 handmade greetings : creative cards and clever correspondence / Laura McFadden.
      p. cm.
  Includes bibliographical references and index.
  ISBN-13: 978-1-59253-473-9
  ISBN-10: 1-59253-473-2
  1. Greeting cards. 2. Stationery. I. Title. II. Title: One thousand
handmade greetings. III. Title: Creative cards and clever correspondence.
  TT872.M33315 2009
  745.594'1--dc22

                                        2008038753
                                        CIP

ISBN-13: 978-1-59253-473-9
ISBN-10: 1-59253-473-2

10 9 8 7 6 5 4 3 2 1

Design: Laura McFadden
Production: Laura McFadden, Deborah Baskin,
Carolynn DeCillo, and Paul DiMattia
Photography: Lightstream

Printed in China

1000

Handmade Greetings

creative cards and
clever correspondence

LAURA MCFADDEN with DEBORAH BASKIN

QUARRY BOOKS

CONTENTS

INTRODUCTION

hello

THESE PAST FEW MONTHS have been like any other, except for one thing—my mail. It's about 4:30 p.m. at my house in Somerville, Massachusetts, and my overzealous Hungarian pointer, Pluto, is barking his head off. The mailman stands on the other side of the oak door and riffles through his bag while my dog gets ready to pounce. Our carrier calmly stuffs as many envelopes as he can fit through the slot, knowing full well he'll be protected from my dog's sharp canines by the wood barrier that lies in between.

I gather up the fallen rectangles from the floor and start to sort. Bills, catalogs, and flyers are left in a heap and ignored as I eagerly tear open the quirky, personalized envelopes with a childlike enthusiasm. They are adorned with beautiful stamps, little drawings, and funky labels. They are submission envelopes for 1,000 *Handmade Greetings*.

Even better is what's inside. Whether it's a block print with some ink that oozes over the edges, or a hand-sewn card with a slightly crooked stitch, these hand-wrought imperfections only enhance the charms of these handmade cards. Making these cards allows the artists to be free and loose, to experiment with whatever materials they want, and to leave a personal touch.

We hope you will find hours, months, and years of inspiration in the enormous collection of cards showcased in *1,000 Handmade Greetings*. We've received entries from all over the world, including North America, Europe, Greece, and as far away as Australia and China. We've selected the cards based on their visual attractiveness, their design concepts, and their innovative use of materials. You will find a wide variety of mediums, styles, and ideas.

I think what's most important to remember is how much pleasure the artists got out of making these cards. I hope this feeling is imparted to you as you flip through the pages of this book.

LAURA MCFADDEN

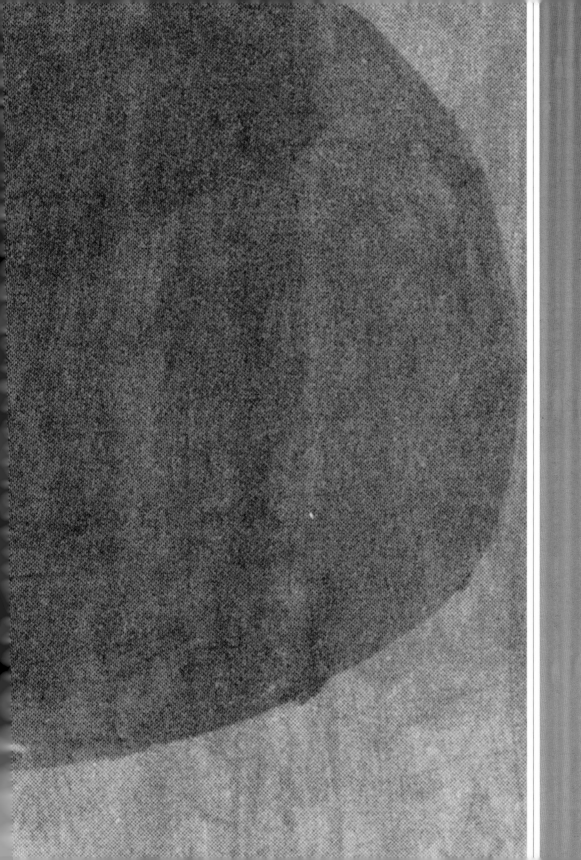

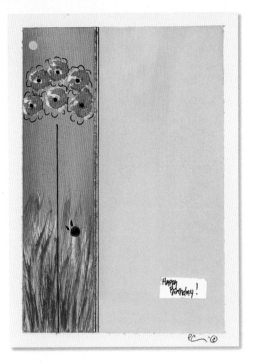

0001 | Peter Ceccarelli for Constance Kay

0002 | Christina Bevilacqua

0003 | Christina Bevilacqua

0004 | Peter Ceccarelli for Constance Kay

0005 | Susy Pilgrim Waters

0006 | Janell Genovese

0007 | Janell Genovese

0008 | Anna Herrick

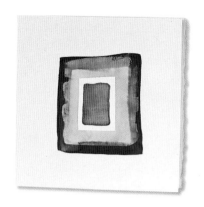

0009 | Anna Herrick

0010 | Anna Herrick

0011 | Anna Herrick

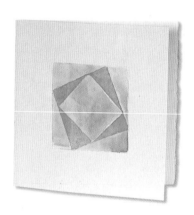

0012 | Anna Herrick

0013 | Anna Herrick

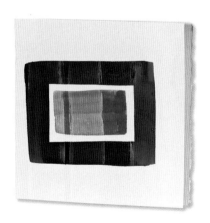

0014 | Anna Herrick

0015 | Anna Herrick

0016 | Anna Herrick

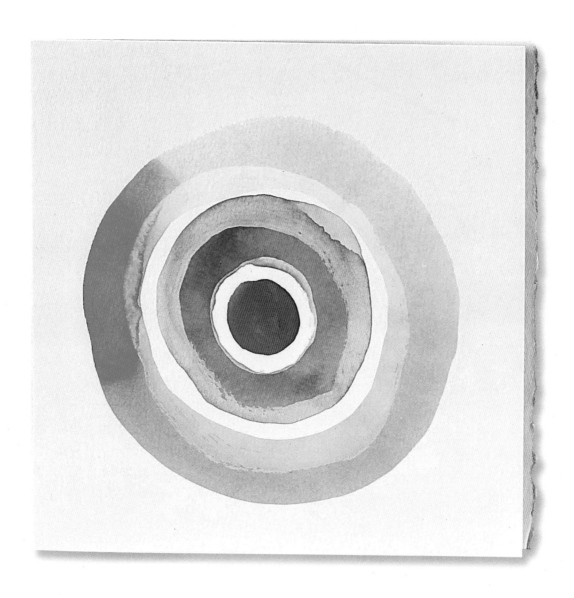

0017 | Anna Herrick

0018 | Kristine A. Lombardi

0019 | Ry Stephens Design

0020 | Kristine A. Lombardi

0021 | Elizabeth Smith for Constance Kay

0022 | Christy Flora

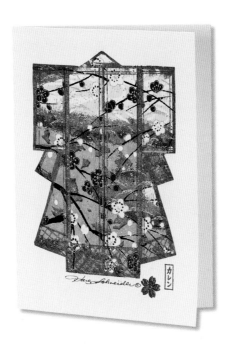

0023 | Karen Schneider for Constance Kay

0024 | Elizabeth Smith for Constance Kay

0025 | Juliah Manjaji for Constance Kay

0026 | Juliah Manjaji for Constance Kay

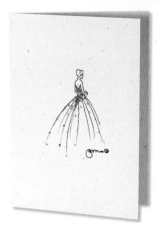

0027 | Juliah Manjaji for Constance Ka

0028 | Juliah Manjaji for Constance Kay

0029 | Amy Stocklein

0030 | Juliah Manjaji for Constance K

0031 | Juliah Manjaji for Constance Kay

0032 | Juliah Manjaji for Constance Kay

0033 | Juliah Manjaji for Constance

0084 | Julie Belcher for Yee-Haw Industries

his.
hers.

0085 | Caite McNeil for Constance Kay

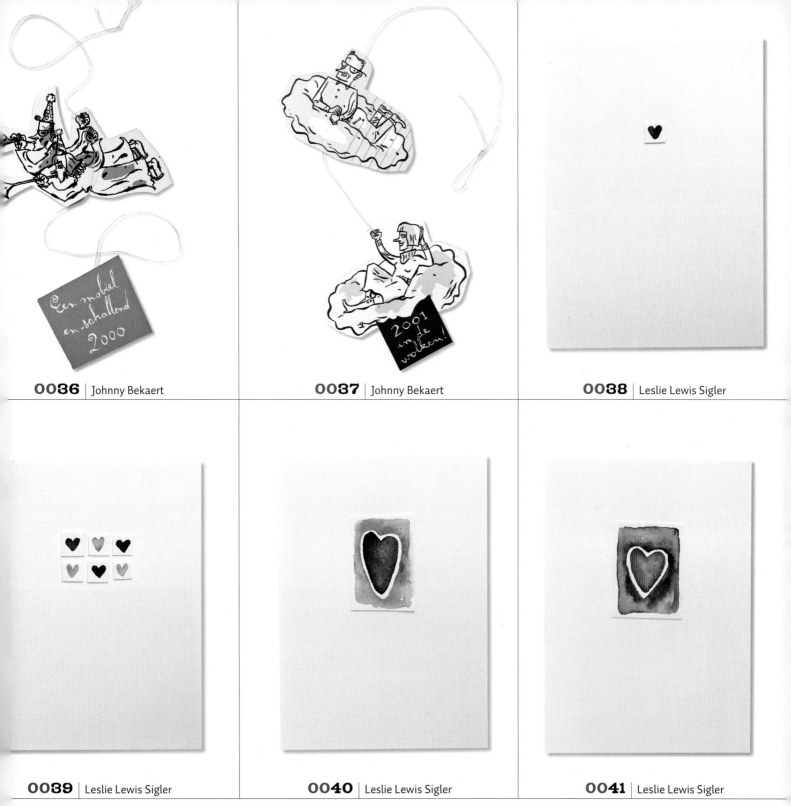

0036 | Johnny Bekaert

0037 | Johnny Bekaert

0038 | Leslie Lewis Sigler

0039 | Leslie Lewis Sigler

0040 | Leslie Lewis Sigler

0041 | Leslie Lewis Sigler

0042 | Alison Blackwell

0043 | Susan Delsandro Hellier

0044 | Sandra McCormick for Constanc

0045 | Jeanine Abels for Constance Kay

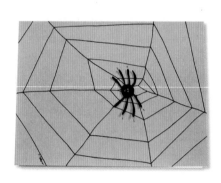

0046 | Christy Flora

0047 | Heather Victoria Held

0048 | Kelly M. King

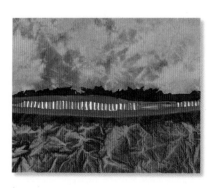

0049 | Jeanine Abels for Constance Kay

0050 | Heather Victoria Held

0053-0054 | Susy Pilgrim Waters

0055 | Johnny Bekaert

0056 | Colleen McLaughlin

0057 | Adolfo Serra

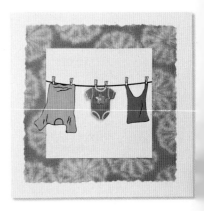

0058 | Daphne Savides & Efi Georgi

0059 | Lisa M. Volz

0060 | Magdalen C. Mowery

0061 | Christy Flora

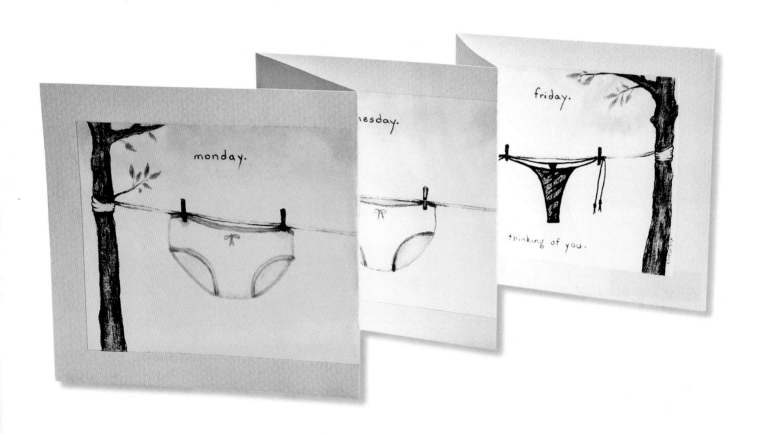

0062 | Leila Singleton

0063 | Claudia Middendorf

0064 | Rodney Durso

0065 | Rodney Durso

0066 | Rodney Durso

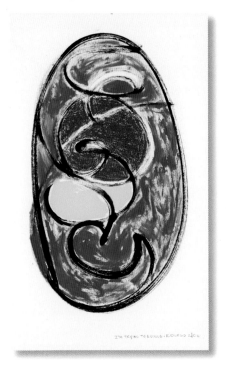

0067 | Rodney Durso

0068 | Mary Tomas for Constance Kay

0069 | Mary Tomas for Constance Kay

0070 | Amy Stocklein

0071 | Give Color

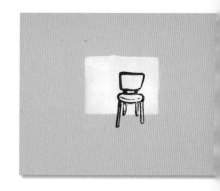

0072 | Amy Stocklein

0073 | Christy Flora

0074 | Jeanmarie Fiocchi-Marden

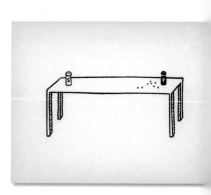

0075 | Paper Cloud

0076 | Sue Jennings for Constance Kay

0077 | Amy Stocklein

0078 | Jennifer Jessee for Yee-Haw Ind

12/16   bARRioS   [signature]

0080 | Liz Adams

0081 | Heidi Burton

0082 | Heidi Burton

0083 | Heather Price

0084 | Alison Blackwell

0085 | Jeanine Abels for Constance Kay

0086 | www.sheriesloane.com

0087 | Betsy Wilson

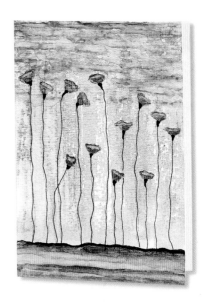

0088 | Darlene Maciuba-Koppel

0089 | www.sheriesloane.com

0090 | Anna Herrick

0091 | Give Color

Fine Art Cards **37**

0092 | Marilla Alexander

0093 | Karla Field

0094 | Marilla Alexander

0095 | Marilla Alexander

0096 | Brenda Zapotosky

0097 | Marilla Alexander

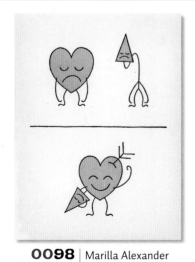

0098 | Marilla Alexander

0099 | Brenda Zapotosky

0100 | Christy Flora

0101 | Karla Field

0102 | Karla Field

0103 | Sarah Roberto

0104-0106 | The Little Anorak Girl

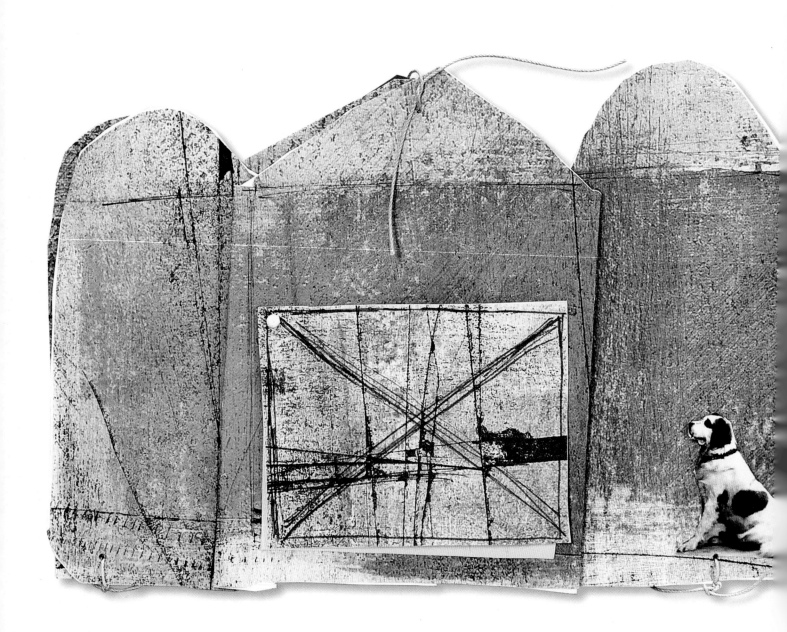

0107 | Linda Solovic

0108 | Linda Solovic

0109 | Linda Solovic

0110 | Linda Solovic

0111 | Heidi B. Lauman

Cherish yesterday, dream tomorrow, live today.

0112 | Stephany Zerbe

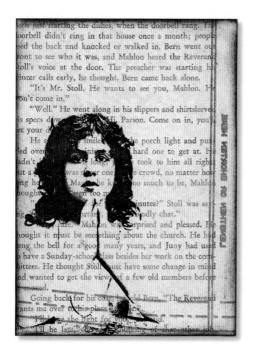

0113 | Shelley Coombes

0114 | Heidi B. Lauman

This page is a collage artwork combining a butterfly illustration over an index page. The index text (columns of place names with reference numbers) and the butterfly form the artwork itself.

...agusta, Cyprus 1200	2	G8	Gerar, Anc. Heb. K.	2	A5	Halys (R.), Bab. Emp.	1	H1
...anum Fortunae, It.	7	J5	Gergithus, Graec.	4	J1	Halys (R.), Egyp. Emp.	1	C1
...aria R., Mod. Pal.	6	Q9	Gerizim, Mt., Anc. Heb. K.	2	C3	Halys (R.), Per. Emp.		D1
...aroe Is., Eur. 1815	2	H7	German Confederation, Eur.			Hamadan, Per. Emp.	3	G3
...aventia, It.	9	B1	1815		E3	Hamath, Egyp. Emp.	1	D2
...eltria, It.	6	P8	Germania, Rom. Emp.	6	D1	Hamath, Bab. Emp.		J2
...ere, Eur. 1810	6	P7	Germanicæ, Anc. Eur.	5	D1	Hamath, Per. Emp.	3	E2
...eronia, It.	8	C2	Gerona, Eur. 1810	8	C2	Hamaxitos, Graec.	4	H2
...errara, Eur. 1810	6	O10	Gerontia (I.) Graec.	4	F2	Hambur... Eur. 1810	8	C1
...errentinum, It.	8	D2	Gerra, Bab. Emp.	1	L4	...amburg, Eur. 1815	9	F3
...ez, N. Afr. 1815	6	Q10	Gerra, Per. Emp.	3	G4	Hammath, Anc. Heb. K.	2	D2
...idan, Wadi, Mod. Pal.	9	B7	Gerræi, The, Bab. Emp.	1	L4	Hannathon, Anc. Heb. K.	2	C2
...ig, Mod. Pal.	2	H9	Gerræ, The, Per. Emp.	3	G...	Hanover, Eur. 1810	8	C1
...inisterre, C., Eur. 1810	2	H7	Geshurites, The, Anc. Heb.			Hanover, Eur. 1815	9	E3
...inland, Eur.		R2	K.		D1	...		H10
...inland, Eur.			...te, Per. Emp.	3	C1	...		G9
...inland, G.			...Anc. Eur.	5		...		J7
...iqra, Wadi			...Mod.			...		J4
...irmum, It.			...ar			...ar		H9
...iume, Eur.						...di		H9
...iume, Eur.			Gib...			...		H6
...laminia, Via			Gib...			...Wadi		G8
...lanaticus Si.,			...			...ta		O8
...levo L., Rom. Em...			...			...		D1
...lorence, Eur. 1200			...nn			...		H8
...lorence, Eur. 1810			...			...Mont. Emp.	6	L4
...lorence, Eur. 1815			...			...It.		Q9
...lorentia, It.			...			...Eur. 1810	8	C2
...okshany, Eur. 1810			...			...Eur. 1815	9	D4
...ontainebleau, Eur. 1810	8		Gin...			...Egyp. Emp	1	C4
...orentum, It.	6		...			...Anc. Heb. K.		C1
...ormiae, It.	6		...sgow			...(Is.), Eur. 1810	8	B1
...ormio Fl., It.	6.		...			...(Is.), Eur. 1815	9	B2
...orun Fulvii, It.	6		...			...Mod. Pal.		H8
...orum Julii, Rom. Emp.	6		...mp.			...Anc. Heb. K.	2	C2
...orum Traiani, It.	6	O1...				...us (R.), Graec.	4	J1
...rance (K.), Eur. 1200	7	C3	...200			...atompylos, Per. Emp.	3	
...rance, Eur. 1810	8	C2				...dan (Wadi), Mod. Pal.		H...
...rance, Eur. 1815	9	D4	...n. Emp.			...eilsberg, Eur. 1810		H...
...ranconia, Eur. 1200	7	D3	Golan, Anc. Heb. K.	2	D2	Heiyani, Wadi, Mod. Pal.		
...rankfurt, Eur. 1810	8	C1	Golan (Ld. of), Anc. Heb. K.	2	D2	Helene vel Macris, Graec.		F...
...rankfurt, Eur. 1815	9	E3	Gomphi, Graec.	4	C2	Helice, Graec.		
...redericia, Eur. 1810	8	C1	Gonnus, Graec.	4	D2	Helicon Mt., Graec.	4	D3
...regellae, It.	6	Q10	Gorditanum Prom., It.	8	O10	Heligoland, Eur. 1810	8	E3
...iegenae, It.	6	Q10	Gordium, Per. Emp.	3	D2	Heligoland, Eur. 1815	9	E3
...reiburg, Eur. 1810	9	E4	Gordyene, Rom. Emp.	6	L4	Heliopolis, Bab. Emp.	1	H3
...rentani, It.		R9	Gortys, Graec.	4	D4	Heliopolis, Egyp. Emp.	1	C3

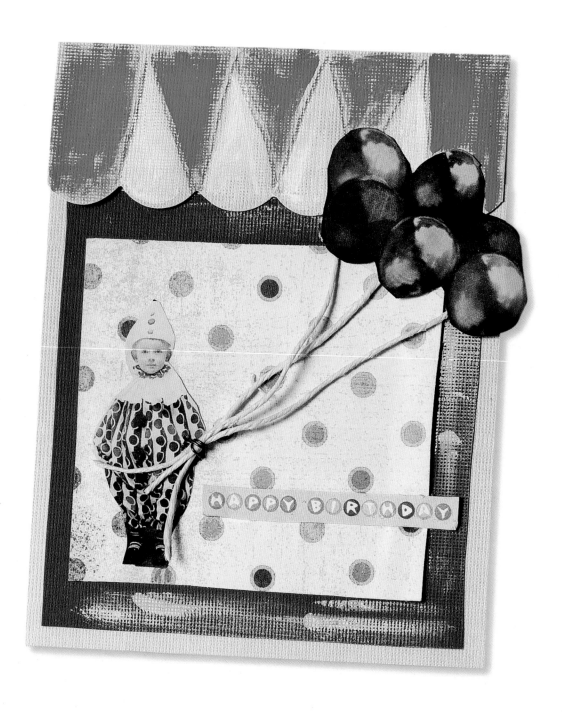

0117 | Tammy Kushnir

0118 | Tammy Kushnir

0119 | Tammy Kushnir

0120 | Tammy Kushnir

0121 | Amy Rowan

0122 | Leila Singleton

0123 | Su-Queen Teo

0124 | Meri Meri Inc

0125 | Christina Bevilacqua

0126 | Susan Delsandro Hellier

0127 | Jeanine Abels for Constance Kay

0128 | Jeanine Abels for Constance Kay

0129 | Michelle Pugh

0180 | Amy Rowan

0181 | Catherine Anson

0132 | Pam Sparks

0133-0135 | Allison Cole

0186 | Joel C. Adamich

0187 | Stephany Zerbe

0188 | Joel C. Adamich

0189 | Joel C. Adamich

0140 | Joel C. Adamich

0141 | Joel C. Adamich

0142 | Joel C. Adamich

0143 | Joel C. Adamich

0144 | Joel C. Adamich

0145 | Stephany Zerbe

i'm nuts about you!

0146 | Victoria Smith for Constance Kay

0147 | Phoebe Wang

0148 | Phoebe Wang

0149 | Phoebe Wang

50 | Suzanne Purnell for Constance Kay

0151 | Victoria Smith for Constance Kay

0152 | Suzanne Purnell for Constance Kay

0153 | Laura McFadden

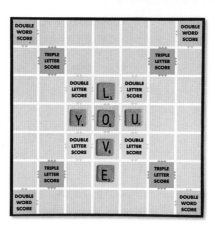

0154 | Laura McFadden

0155 | Susan Delsandro Hellier

0156 | Laura McFadden

0157 | Laura McFadden

0158 | Laura McFadden

0159 | Meri Meri Inc

0160 | Katie Lipsitt

0161 | Laura McFadden

0162 | Su-Queen Teo

0164 | RePlayGround

0165 | Lea Cioci CPD CPT

0166 | Katie Lipsitt

0167 | Trudy Lopez for Constance Kay

0168 | Pam Sparks

0169 | Renee Goetz for Constance Kay

0170 | Rosemary Buczek for Constance

0171 | Christine Reising

0172 | Kim White-Jenkins

0173 | Ellen G. Horovitz

0174 | Penny Craig for Constance Kay

0175 | Ellen G. Horovitz

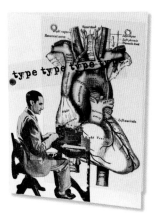

0176 | Kim White-Jenkins

0177 | Ellen G. Horovitz

0178 | Meri Meri Inc

0179 | Meri Meri Inc

0180 | Meri Meri Inc

0183 | Tai Stith

0184 | Tai Stith

0185 | Tai Stith

0186 | Tai Stith

0187 | Tai Stith

0188 | Tai Stith

0189 | Fela Ife Cortés for Babas2nd Design

0190 | Fela Ife Cortés for Babas2nd Design

0191 | Fela Ife Cortés for Babas2nd Design

0192 | Fela Ife Cortés for Babas2nd Design

0193 | Fela Ife Cortés for Babas2nd Design

0194 | Brian Kenny

0195 | Cheryl Rotnem

0196 | Brian Kenny

0197 | Roger That!

0198 | Roger That!

0199 | Leah Daehling

0200 | Roger That!

0201 | Brian Kenny

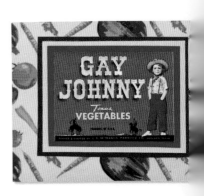

0202 | Brian Kenny

0203 | Katie Lipsitt

i forgot

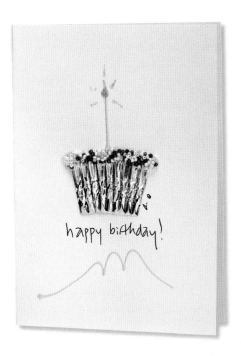

0205 | Christie Wood for Constance Kay

0206 | Penny Craig for Constance Kay

0207 | Victoria Smith for Constance Kay

0208 | Victoria Smith for Constance Kay

0209 | Susan Delsandro Hellier

0210 | Angela Liguori

0211 | Angela Liguori

0212 | Meri Meri Inc

0213 | Karin Winter

0214 | Daphne Savides & Efi Georg

0215 | Laura McFadden

0216 | Susan Delsandro Hellier

0217 | Karin Winter

0218 | Ines Madurga Martin-Serrano

0220 | Meri Meri Inc

0221 | Meri Meri Inc

0222 | Meri Meri Inc

0223 | Meri Meri Inc

0224 | Meri Meri Inc

0225 | Meri Meri Inc

0226 | Meri Meri Inc

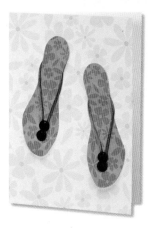

0227 | Meri Meri Inc

0228 | Meri Meri Inc

0229 | Meri Meri Inc

0230 | Meri Meri Inc

0231 | Meri Meri Inc

0232 | Meri Meri Inc

0233 | Meri Meri Inc

0234 | Meri Meri Inc

0237 | Meri Meri Inc

0238 | Meri Meri Inc

0239 | Meri Meri Inc

0240 | Meri Meri Inc

0241 | Meri Meri Inc

0242 | Meri Meri Inc

0243 | Jenn Mason

0244 | Meri Meri Inc

0245 | Meri Meri Inc

0246 | Meri Meri Inc

0247 | Meri Meri Inc

0248 | Meri Meri Inc

0249 | Meri Meri Inc

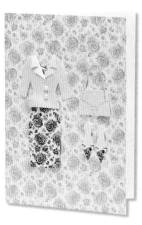

0250 | Meri Meri Inc

0251 | Meri Meri Inc

0253-0254 | Kelci Gonzalez

0255 | Colleen Penn

0256 | Cheryl Rotnem

0257 | Moderncard

0258 | Trudy Lopez for Constance Kay

0259 | Tracie L. Brown

0260 | Tracie L. Brown

Maria
wished
for
world
peace

and better bangs.

0262 | Alicia Holland

0263 | Meri Meri Inc

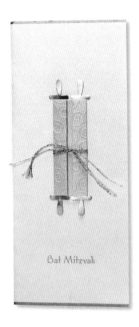

0264 | Meri Meri Inc

0265 | Stelie Designs

0266 | Meri Meri Inc

0267 | Brian Kenny

0268 | Verandah Times

0269 | Verandah Times

0270 | Verandah Times

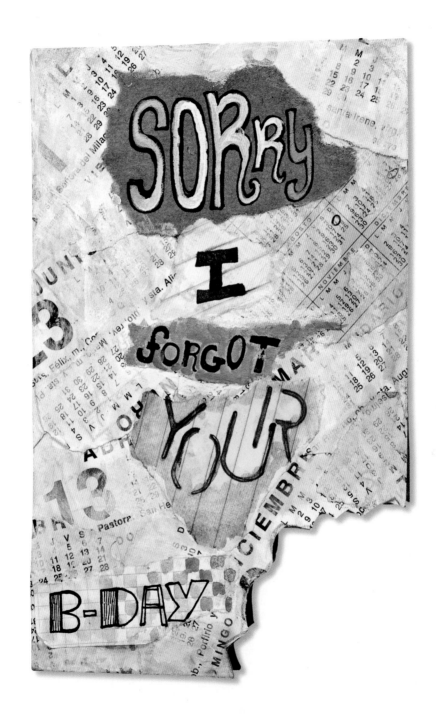

0272 | Lisa Kettell

0273 | Lisa Kettell

0274 | Holly A. Stinnett

0275 | Holly A. Stinnett

0276 | Holly A. Stinn

0277 | Brian Kenny

tear or fold along this line and keep as bookmark

0278 | Lara Captan for Leila Amad Bissat

79 | Musfy & Captan for Leila Amad Bissat

0280 | Musfy & Captan for Leila Amad Bissat

0281 | Suzanne Kinstle Nocera

2 | Musfy & Captan for Leila Amad Bissat

0283 | Musfy & Captan for Leila Amad Bissat

0284 | Suzanne Kinstle Nocera

0285 | Heather Crossley

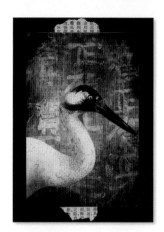

0286 | Angela Platten

0287 | Lea Cioci CPD CPT

0288 | Heather Crossley

0289 | Tai Stith

0290 | Heather Crossley

0291 | Heather Crossley

0292 | D. Matzen

0293 | Angela Platten

0294 | Heather Crossley

0295 | Martha Starke

0296 | Martha Starke

0297 | Martha Starke

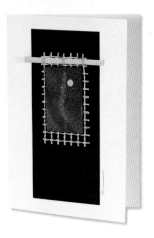

0299 | Sandra Moen for Constance Kay

0300 | Lynne Garell

0301 | Laurie Strong

0302 | Lea Cioci

0303 | Michelle Biscotti

0304 | Heather Crossley

0305 | Karen McCann

0306 | Katie Lipsitt

0307 | Kay Nelson for Constance K

0308 | Stephany Zerbe

0309 | Miss Lyn Cardinal

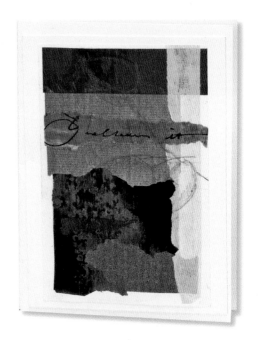

0310 | Miss Lyn Cardinal

0311 | Miss Lyn Cardinal

0312 | Miss Lyn Cardinal

a series of impressions

my love for yo...
is a journey;
starting at forever,
and ending at nev...
-Anony...

0818 | Stephaie McAtee

0814 | Kerry Clarke

0815 | Heather Grow

0816 | Heather Grow

0817 | Loretta D'Onofrio

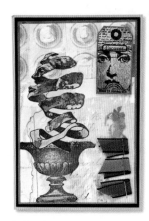

0818 | Loretta D'Onofrio

0819 | Loretta D'Onofrio

0820 | Loretta D'Onofrio

0821 | Loretta D'Onofrio

0822 | Loretta D'Onofrio

WHAT'S IN STORE

an Aegean blue sea, the next it's It...
most romantic city. Wherever you are...
no better place to sit back and w...

0323 | Lea Cioci CPD CPT

0324 | Desert Mtn Designs by Pammaro

0325 | Meri Meri Inc

0326 | Meri Meri Inc

0327 | Victoria Cole

0328 | Meri Meri Inc

0329 | Andrea M. Amu

0330 | Meri Meri Inc

0331 | Victoria Smith for Constance Kay

0332 | Meri Meri Inc

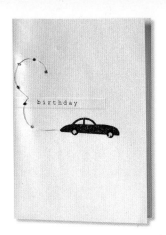

0333 | Meri Meri Inc

0334 | Meri Meri Inc

0335 | Sandra Moen for Constance Kay

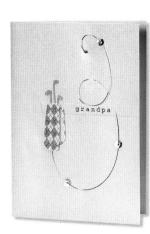

0336 | Meri Meri Inc

0337 | Meri Meri Inc

0338 | Merlyn Bost for Constance Kay

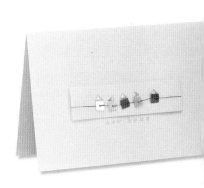

0339 | Meri Meri Inc

You shall go to the Ball...

0340 | Meri Meri Inc

0842 | Maricel V. Fabi

0843 | Meri Meri Inc

0844 | Lana Kecovich

0845 | Meri Meri Inc

0846 | Guadalupe Barceló-Helmig

0847 | Moderncard

0848 | Lana Kecovich

0849 | Laura McFadden

0850 | Cassie Heist

0351 | Meri Meri Inc

0352 | Meri Meri Inc

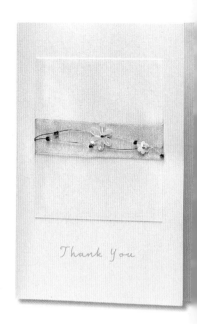

0353 | Meri Meri Inc

0354 | Meri Meri Inc

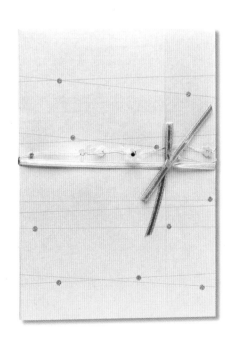

0355 | Meri Meri Inc

0356 | Meri Meri Inc

0357 | Meri Meri Inc

0358 | Meri Meri Inc

Relax, it's your Birthday!

0359 | Meri Meri Inc

0360 | Meri Meri Inc

...congratulations on your retirement!

0361 | Meri Meri Inc

0362 | Meri Meri Inc

0363 | Meri Meri Inc

0364 | Meri Meri Inc

0365 | Meri Meri Inc

0366 | Meri Meri Inc

0367 | Meri Meri Inc

0368 | Meri Meri Inc

0369 | Meri Meri Inc

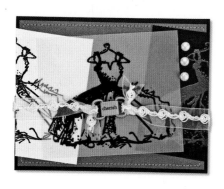

0370 | Ruthann Reikes

0371 | Amy Moore / Enfleur

0372 | Jennifer Rewitz

0373 | Meri Meri Inc

0374 | Meri Meri Inc

0375 | Katie Lipsitt

0376 | Meri Meri Inc

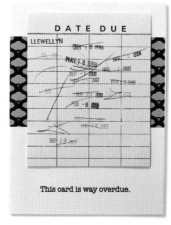

0377 | Cracked Designs LLC

0378 | Tai Stith

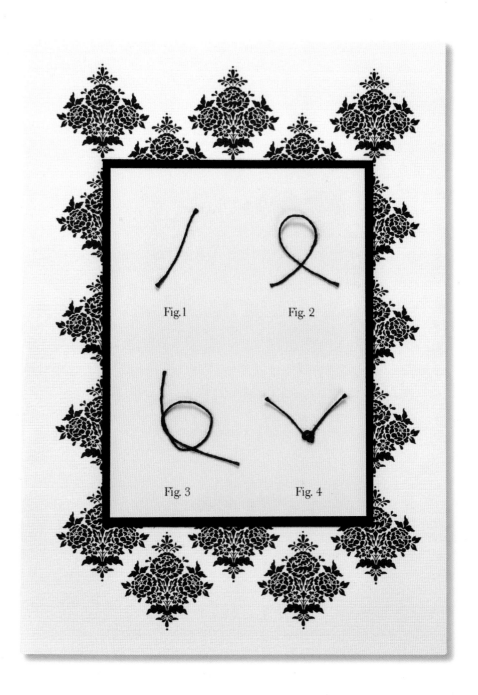

Fig. 1

Fig. 2

Fig. 3

Fig. 4

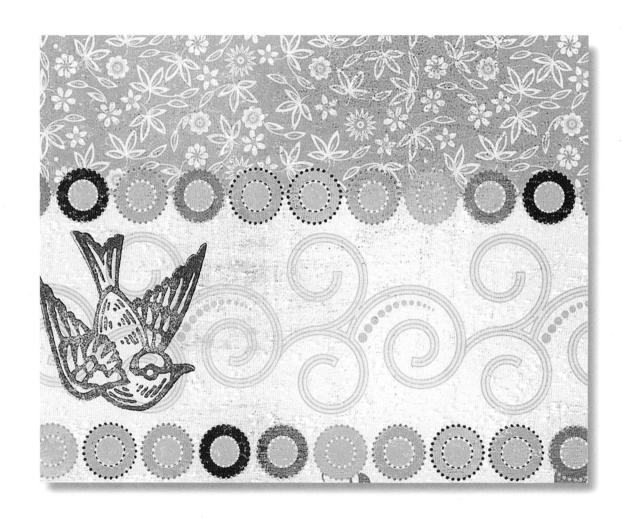

0381 | Katie Lipsitt

0382 | Teresa Espinosa

0383 | Teresa Espinosa

0384 | Lynne Garell

0385 | Lisa Sorrentino

0386 | Barbara Bourassa

0387 | Pam Das

0388 | Susan Ure for Constance Kay

0389 | Donna Sutor for Constance K

0390 | Pam Das

0391 | Sandra Moen for Constance Kay

0392 | Donna Sutor for Constance

0393 | Donna Sutor for Constance Kay

0394 | Sandra Moen for Constance Kay

0395 | Sandra Moen for Constance

0396 | Pam Das

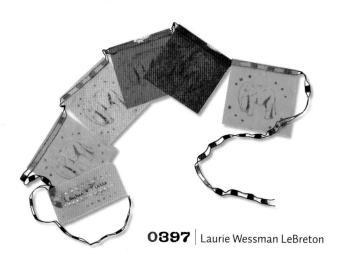

0397 | Laurie Wessman LeBreton

0898 | Laurie Wessman LeBreton

399 | Sharon Prince for Constance Kay

0400 | Meri Meri Inc

0401 | Fela Ife Cortés

402 | Annie Weiner for Constance Kay

0403 | Anna Herrick

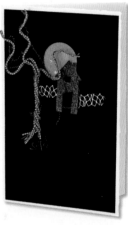

0404 | Donna Sutor Constance Kay

05 | Danielle Engwert for Constance Kay

0406 | Anna Herrick

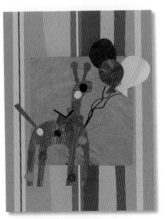

0407 | Sarah Kelly, Spadazzle

0408 | Odonata Press

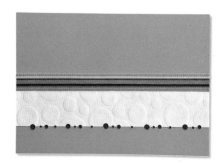

0409 | Niki Collins

0410 | Maggie Hallam

0411 | Susan Ure for Constance Kay

0412 | Niki Collins

0413 | Colleen Penn

0414 | Susan Ure for Constance Kay

0415 | Brian Kenny

0416 | Anna Herrick

0417 | Jenn Mason

0418 | Susy Pilgrim Waters

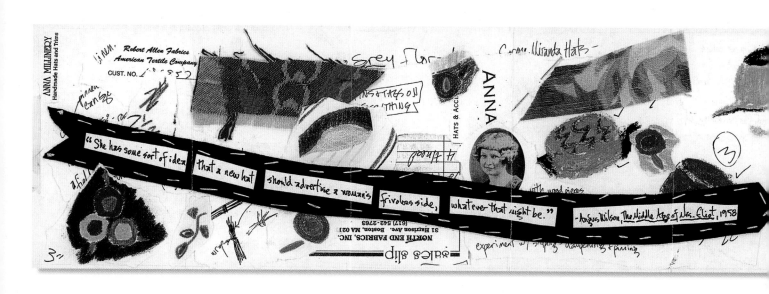

0419 | Christina Bevilacqua

0420 | A Punkin Card Company

0422 | Susy Pilgrim Waters

0421 | Sara Simpson

0423 | Lynne Garell

0424 | Katie Lipsitt

0425 | Katie Lipsitt

0426 | Michelle Pugh

0427 | Laura McFadden

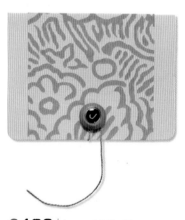

0428 | Laura McFadden

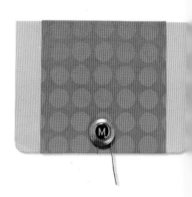

0429 | Laura McFadden

0430 | Laura McFadden

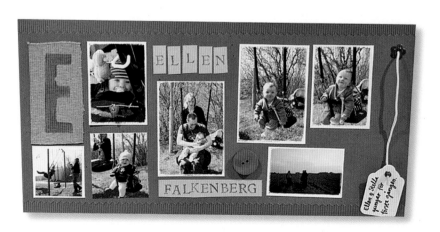

0431 | Linda Pabst

0432-0433 | Laura McFadden

HAPPY VALENTINES DAY

0434 | Love Dog Card Company

0435 | Meri Meri Inc

0436 | Palmarosa Hand Crafts

Secret Admirer

0437 | Love Dog Card Company

0438 | Brian Kenny

Danke Schoen

0439 | Brian Kenny

0440 | Brian Kenny

I'll vote for this roll of toilet paper before I vote Republican!

0441 | Roger That!

TOXIC
Love

0442 | Love Dog Card Company

0443 | Brian Kenny

3 | HAND-PRINTED, STAMPED & STENCILED CARDS

0444 | Give Color

0445 | Give Color

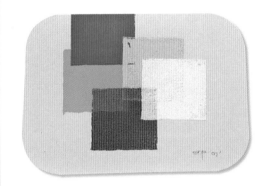

0446 | Give Color

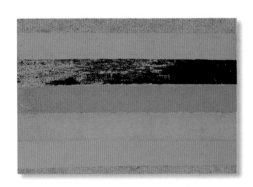

0447 | Give Color

0448 | Give Color

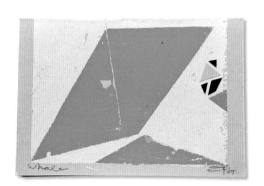

0449 | Give Color

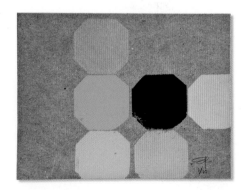

0450 | Give Color

0451 | Keri Straus

0452 | Give Color

0453 | Peng Peng Klayman

0454 | Keri Straus

0455 | Verandah Times

0456 | Caitlin Keegan

0457 | Keri Straus

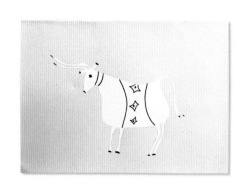

0458 | Verandah Times

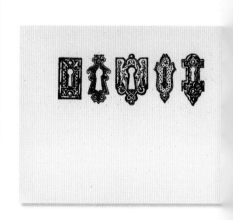

0459 | Keri Straus

OUR TREE IS BIGGER

0461 | Jeanmarie Fiocchi-Marden

0462 | Jenskelley.com

0463 | Jenskelley.com

0464 | Jenskelley.com

0465 | Jenskelley.com

0466 | Verandah Times

0467 | Jenskelley.com

0468 | Jennifer Schildt

0469 | Robline Forsythe

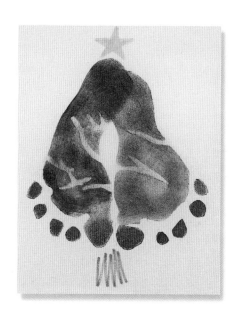

0470 | Barbara Fiocchi

0471 | Denise Johnson

0472 | Melissa Langer

0474 | Maureen O'Connor

0475 | Robline Forsythe

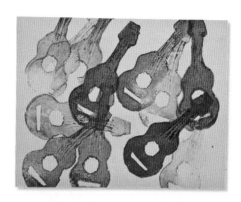

0476 | Palmarosa Hand Crafts

0477 | Katherine Ahn

0478 | Joel C. Adamich

Art washes away from the soul the dust of everyday life.
PICASSO

0479 | Colleen Penn

0480 | Give Color

0481 | Sean Star Wars for Yee-Haw Industries

thank YOU

0482 | Danielle Ameling

0483 | Robline Forsythe

0486 | Jenskelley.com

0487 | Jennifer Schildt

0488 | Victoria Cole

0489 | Verandah Times

0490 | Victoria Cole

0491 | Ellen Rooney

0492 | L. Carol Christopher

0493 | Helen Musselwhite

0494 | Helen Musselwhite

0495 | Helen Musselwhite

0496 | Helen Musselwhite

0497 | easycutpopup.com

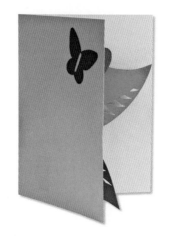

0498 | Karin Marlett Choi

0499 | Love Dog Card Company

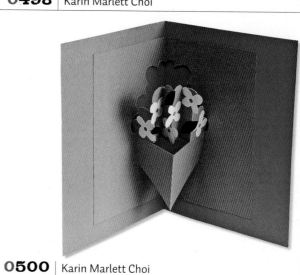

0500 | Karin Marlett Choi

0501 | Ann Martin

0502 | Karin Marlett Choi

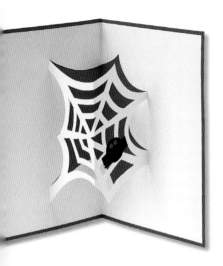

0505 | Tracy Chong

0506 | Tracy Chong

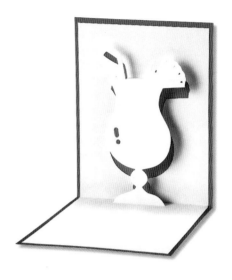

0507 | Tracy Chong

0508 | Tracy Chong

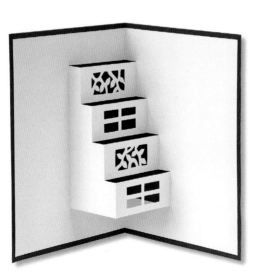

0509 | Tracy Chong

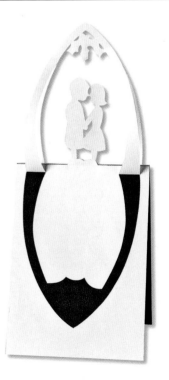

0510 | Tracy Chong

0512-0514 | Alisha Gould Designs

0515 | Laboratory5

0516 | Laboratory5

0517 | Laboratory5

0518 | Laboratory5

0519 | Laboratory5

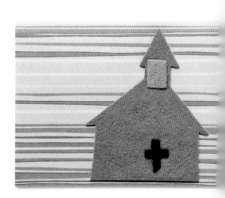

0520 | Laboratory5

0521 | Laboratory5

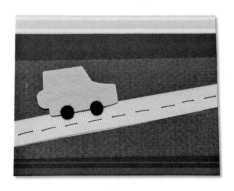

0522 | Laboratory5

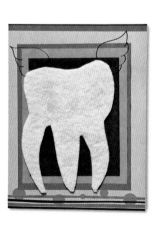

0523 | Laboratory5

0524 | Laboratory5

0525 | Norma V. Toraya

0526 | Norma V. Toraya

0527 | Laura McFadden

0528 | Helen Musselwhite

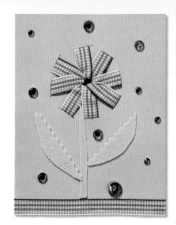

0529 | Laura McFadden

0530 | Sara Stein

0531 | Laura McFadden

0532 | Sara Stein

0533 | Laura McFadden

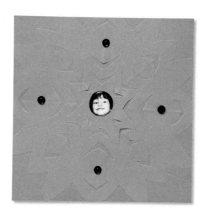

0534 | Laura McFadden

0585 | Laura McFadden

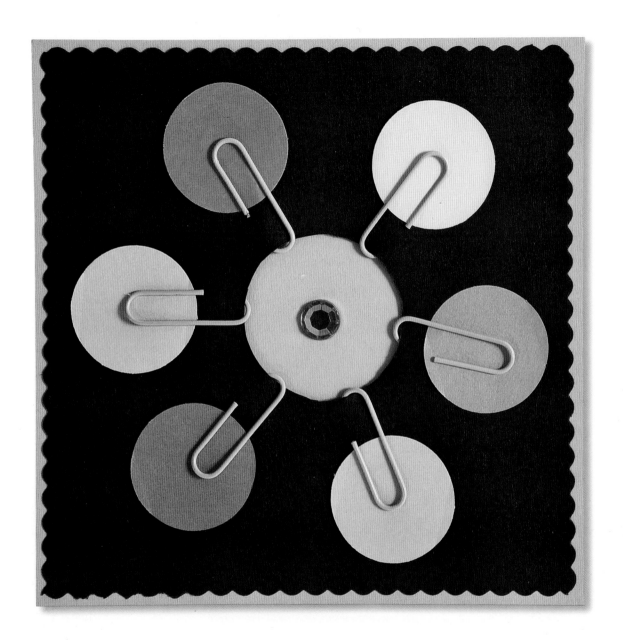

0536 | Laura McFadden

0587 | Claire Sun-ok Choi

0588 | Claire Sun-ok Choi

0539 | Claire Sun-ok Choi

0540 | Claire Sun-ok Choi

0541 | Claire Sun-ok Choi

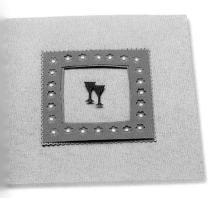

0542 | Claire Sun-ok Choi

0543 | Claire Sun-ok Choi

0544 | Claire Sun-ok Choi

0545 | Claire Sun-ok Choi

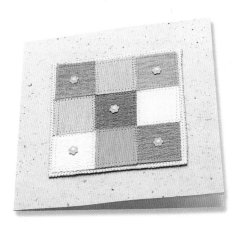

0546 | Claire Sun-ok Choi

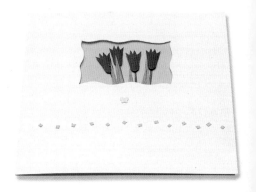

0547 | Claire Sun-ok Choi

0548 | Laboratory5

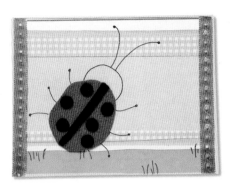

0549 | Laboratory5

0550 | Laboratory5

0551 | Laboratory5

0552 | Laboratory5

0553 | Laboratory5

0554 | Laboratory5

0555 | Laboratory5

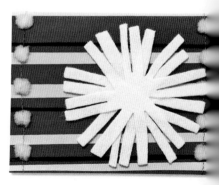

0556 | Laboratory5

0557 | Laboratory5

0558-0559 | Maggie Lamarre

0560 | Meri Meri Inc

THE INCREDIBLE STRETCH TO FIT

ONE SIZE FITS ALL

BOOSH JECKETTA

JUST POP IN THE TURBO BOOSTER STRETCH MAKING DEVICE

0561 | Amy Wallace

0562 | Allyson Nickowitz Ross

0563 | Jan Carp

0564 | Jill Berry

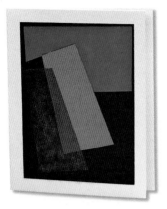

0565 | Anna Herrick

0566 | Anna Herrick

0567 | Amy Wallace

0568 | Allyson Nickowitz Ross

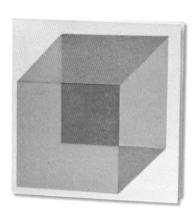

0569 | Anna Herrick

0570 | Anna Herrick

0571 | Caroline Soer

0572 | Hilary Pfeifer for Constance Kay

0573 | Merlyn Bost for Constance Ka

0574 | Christina Bevilacqua

0575 | Claire Sun-ok Choi

0576 | Claire Sun-ok Choi

0577 | Jeanette Imer

0578 | Moderncard

0579 | Angela Liguori

0580 | Ann Martin

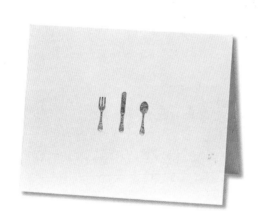

0581 | Moderncard

0582 | Tiffin Mills

0583 | Ann Martin

0584 | Anna Herrick

0585 | Ann Martin

0586 | Angela Liguori

HAPPY BIRTHDAY

hot dog!

0588 | Jenn Mason

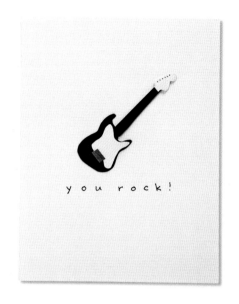

you rock!

0589 | Jenn Mason

just a note!

0590 | Jenn Mason

I ♥ snail mail.

0591 | Ahnalee Brincks

I ♥ snail mail.

0592 | Ahnalee Brincks

I ♥ snail mail.

0593 | Ahnalee Brincks

0594 | Sue Jennings for Constance Kay

0595 | Claire Sun-ok Choi

CHRISTMAS
Cheer

0596 | Charlotte Canup

LOVE

0597 | Christina Williams

0600 | Leslie Lewis Sigler

0601 | Leslie Lewis Sigler

0602 | Leslie Lewis Sigler

0603 | Leslie Lewis Sigler

0604 | Leslie Lewis Sigler

0605 | Leslie Lewis Sigler

0606 | Helen Musselwhite

0607 | Punkahontas

0608 | Helen Musselwhite

0609 | Helen Musselwhite

0610 | Punkahontas

0611 | Punkahontas

0612 | Helen Musselwhite

0613 | Karin Marlett Choi

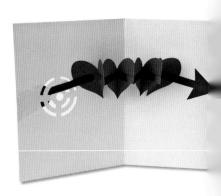

0614 | Karin Marlett Choi

nothing is ever just black & white

0615 | Laura Campbell

0616 | Elizabeth Walsh

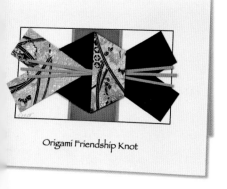

Origami Friendship Knot

0619 | Eve B. Brown

0620 | Melanie Cerajewski

0621 | Eve B. Brown

2 | Bella Tchaitchian for Constance Kay

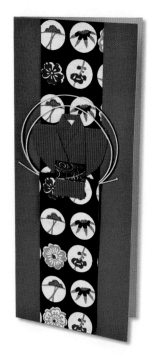

0623 | Eve B. Brown

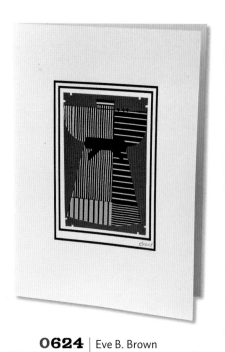

0624 | Eve B. Brown

0625 | Pam Sparks

0626 | Hilary Pfeifer for Constance Kay

0627 | Victoria Smith for Constance

0628 | Stelie Designs

0629 | Dianne D. Tilmann

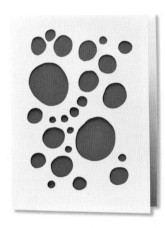

0630 | Marnie B. Karger

0631 | Ursula Wilson for Constance Kay

0632 | Penny Craig for Constance Kay

0633 | Karen Schneider for Constan

0634 | Ellen Jantzen

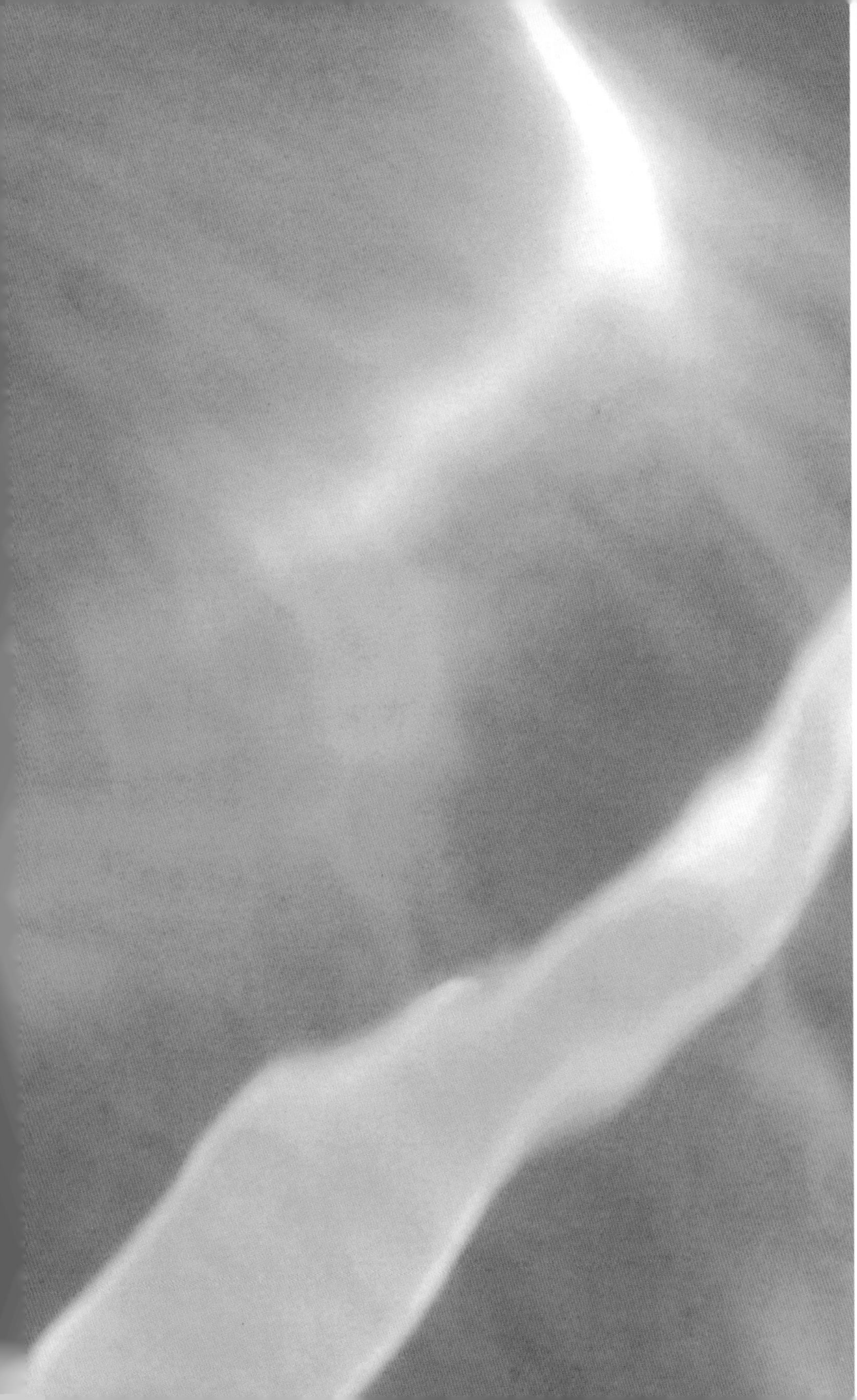

5 PHOTOGRAPHIC CARDS

0635 | House of Six Cats

0636 | House of Six Cats

0637 | House of Six Cats

0688 | Palmarosa Hand Crafts

0639 | House of Six Cats

0640 | Catherine Gibb

0641-0643 | Catherine Gibb

0644 | Karin Winter

0645 | Kari MacKenzie-Bergstrom for Constance Kay

0646 | Kari MacKenzie-Bergstrom for Constance Kay

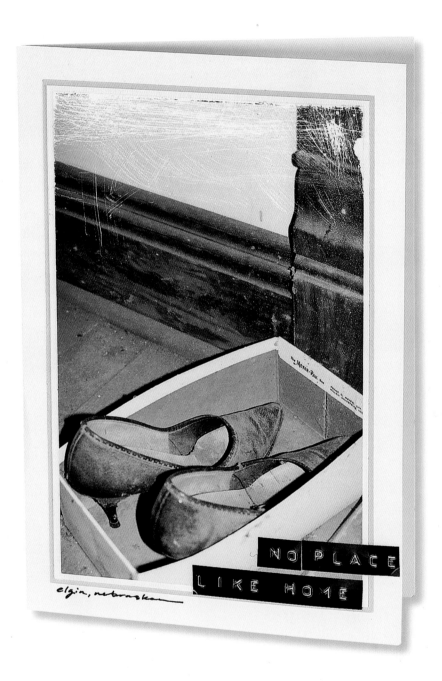

0647 | Leah Daehling

0648 | Paper Stories

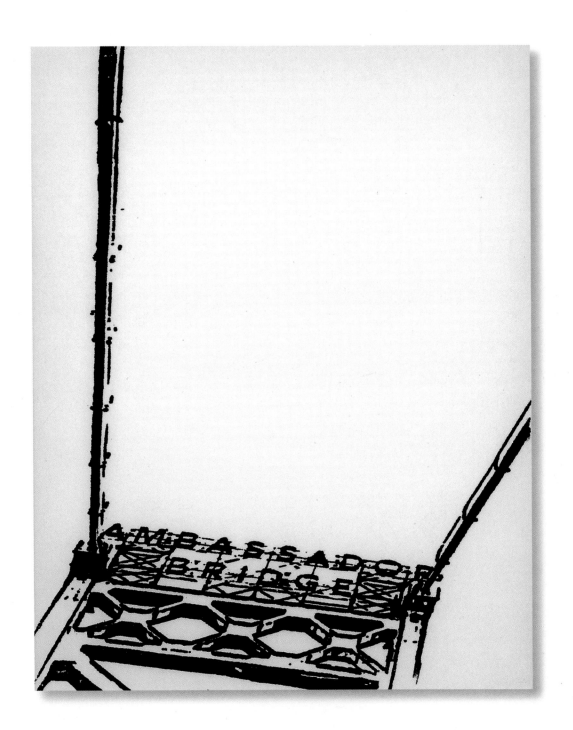

0649 | Paper Stories

O650 | Catherine Gibb

0651 | Laura McFadden

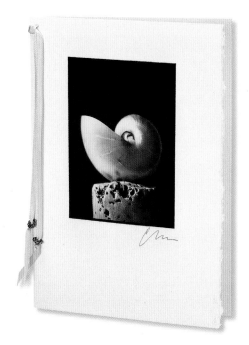

0652 | Claudia Meyer-Newman for Constance Kay

0653 | Mahtab Habibian & Jake Watling

0654 | Claudia Meyer-Newman for Constance Kay

0655 | Joel C. Adamich

0656 | Catherine Gibb

'TIS ROUND.

JcA © 2006

0657 | Joel C. Adamich

0658 | Richard Tuschman

0659 | Gina Phillips

0660 | Stacey Winters

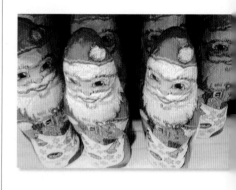

0661 | Mahtab Habibian & Jake Wat

0662 | Gina Phillips

0663 | Gina Phillips

0664 | Gina Phillips

0665 | Stacey Winters

blessed motto

0666 | Ellen G. Horovitz

San José de Gracia, La Trampas, XM

0667 | Joel C. Adamich

San José de Gracia, Las Trampas, NM

0668 | Joel C. Adamich

"San José de Gracia" Las Trampas, N.M.

0669 | Joel C. Adamich

0670 | Carolynn DeCillo

0671 | Carolynn DeCillo

0672 | Carolynn DeCillo

0673 | Carolynn DeCillo

0674 | Carolynn DeCillo

0675 | Joel C. Adamich

Somewhere In Between.   JCA ©2003

0676 | Joel C. Adamich

SURFER'S SHOWER

VcA © 2001

0677 | Joel C. Adamich

Racing, Pueblo Co   Jen ©2001

0678 | Joel C. Adamich

0679 | Joel C. Adamich

0680 | Noah J. Orr Photography

0681 | Joel C. Adamich

Happy Halloween.

0682 | Joel C. Adamich

0683 | Megan Dortch for Empty George

0684 | Milly E. Itzhak

0685 | Amy Stocklein

PEACE ON EARTH

0686 | Pink Bathtub Designs

0689 | Small Screen Designs

0690 | Pinecone + Chickadee

0691 | Jenskelley.com

0692 | Jenskelley.com

0693 | Jenskelley.com

0694 | Amy Rowan

0695 | Pinecone + Chickadee

0696 | Jenskelley.com

0697 | Melanie Schultz

0698 | Melanie Schultz

0699 | Melanie Schultz

0700 | Give Color

0701 | Give Color

0702 | Give Color

0703 | Amy Rowan

0704 | Sarah Parrott

0705 | Sarah Parrott

0706 | Colleen McLaughlin

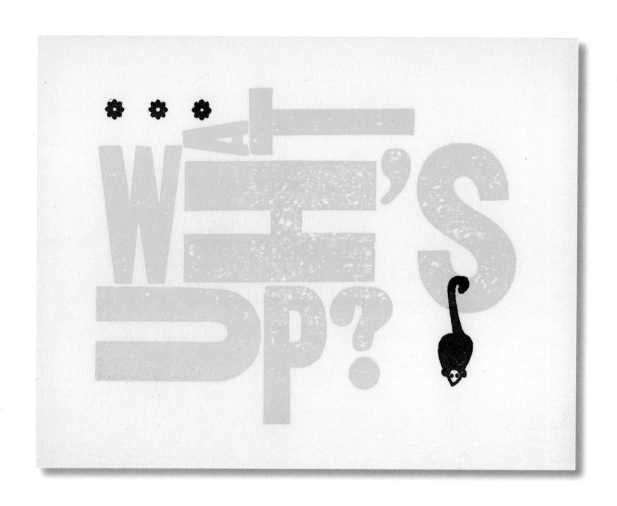

0707 | Amy Stocklein

0708 | Jenni Ohnstad

MERRY CHRISTMAS

0709 | Design des Troy

0710 | Leila Singleton

0711 | Beau Ideal Editions

0712 | Caitlin Keegan

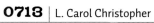

0713 | L. Carol Christopher

0714 | Maggie Hallam

0715 | Maeve Rogers

0716 | Pinecone + Chickadee

0717 | Kala Varner

0718 | Heather Price

0719 | ouou

0720 | ouou

0721 | Sarah Parrott

0722 | Blue Snail Papers

0723 | Mary Kate Thurman

0724 | L. Carol Christopher

0725 | Blue Snail Papers

0726 | Sarah Parrott

0727 | Jenni Ohnstad

0728 | Gillian Beck

0729 | Mary Kate Thurman

0730 | Zoetropa

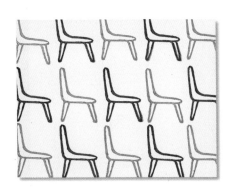

0731 | Zoetropa

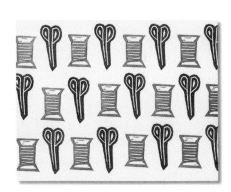

0732 | Zoetropa

0733 | Zoetropa

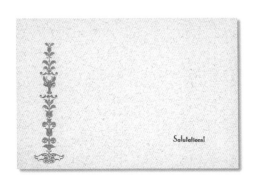

0734 | Maeve Rogers

0735 | Sarah Parrott

0736 | Jackie Carpenter

0737 | Milly E. Itzhak

0738 | Justin Leatherman

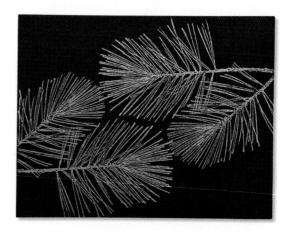

0739 | Sarah Parrott

0740 | Amy Rowan

0741 | Chris Corneal, Lindsay Corneal & Jill Greene

0742 | Karena Colquhoun

Nº 1 2 7/200   "STUFF Nº1"   KARENA '07

0748 | Karena Colquhoun

0744 | Mary Kate Thurman

0745 | Megan Dortch for Empty George

Thank You

0746 | Chiung Hui Juan

Thank You

0747 | Chiung Hui Juan

Thank You

0748 | Chiung Hui Juan

You're Da' Bomb!

0749 | Mary Kate Thurman

0750 | nateduval.com

0751 | nateduval.com

awesome!

0752 | Mary Kate Thurman

hello

0753 | Bjorn Rune Lie for Yee-Haw Industries

0754 | Bjorn Rune Lie for Yee-Haw Industries

0755 | Bjorn Rune Lie for Yee-Haw Industries

0756 | Bjorn Rune Lie for Yee-Haw Industries

0757-0760 | Bjorn Rune Lie for Yee-Haw Industries

0761 | Tamara Galiano

0762 | Bjorn Rune Lie for Yee-Haw Industries

0763 | Two Birds Press, S & T Fisk

0764 | Tamara Galiano

0765-0767 | Julie Belcher for Yee-Haw Industries

0768 | Erica Barraca

0769 | Adam Ewing for Yee-Haw Industries

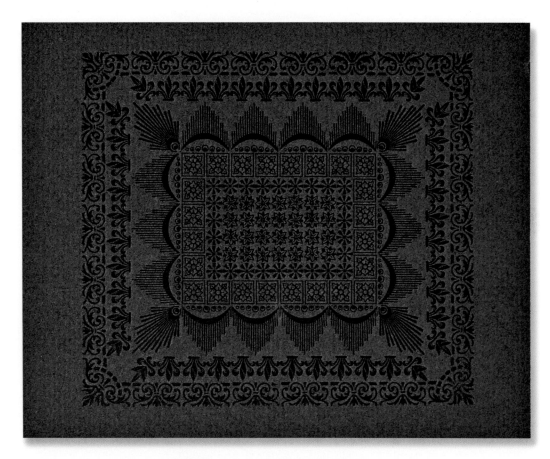

0770 | Two Birds Press, S & T Fisk

0771-0773 | Lizard Press

0774 | Angela Liguori

0775 | Modern Radar

0776 | Modern Radar

0777 | Modern Radar

0778 | Modern Radar

0779 | Modern Radar

0780 | 12fifteen

0781 | Modern Radar

0782 | Amy Rowan

0783 | Lisa Zuraw

0784 | Lisa Zuraw

0785 | Sycamore Street Press

0786 | Jeanette Imer

0787 | Sycamore Street Press

0788 | Denise Johnson

0789 | 12fifteen

0790 | Amy Stocklein

0791 | Lisa Zuraw

0792 | Amy Rowan

3 | Bjorn Rune Lie for Yee-Haw Industires

0794 | Joie Studio / Shop Toast

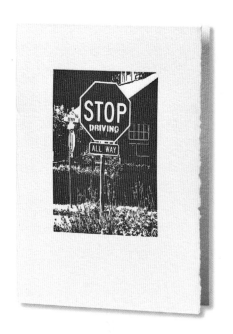

0795 | Lizard Press

96 | Jim Flora for Yee-Haw Industriies

0797 | Bjorn Rune Lie for Yee-Haw Industires

0798 | 12fifteen

boycott
traditional
thought.

0799 | Joel C. Adamich

I love you.

0800 | Joie Studio

happy holidays
peace on earth
warm wishes
joy to the world
season's greetings

0801 | Joie Studio

in my next life
i want to come
back as me.

0802 | Joel C. Adamich

holidaygreetings.

0808 | Erica Barraca

0805 | Gleena.com

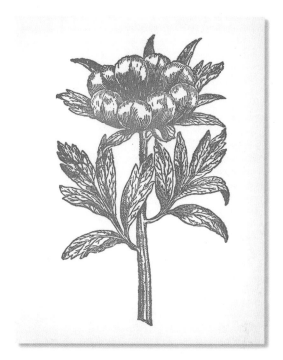

0806 | Gleena.com

0807 | Gleena.com

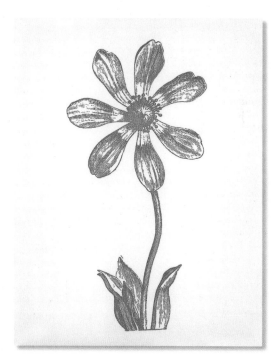

0808 | Gleena.com

0809 | Joie Studio

e-mail has
no soul.

0810 | Joel C. Adamich

hello.

0811 | Michael Neff for Specimen

0812 | Lizard Press

0813 | Lizard Press

0814 | Lizard Press

HAPPY HANUKKAH

0815 | Design des Troy

HAPPY HOLIDAYS

0816 | Amy Stocklein

muchas gracias.

0817 | Erica Barraca

0818 | Paper Stories

0819 | Paper Stories

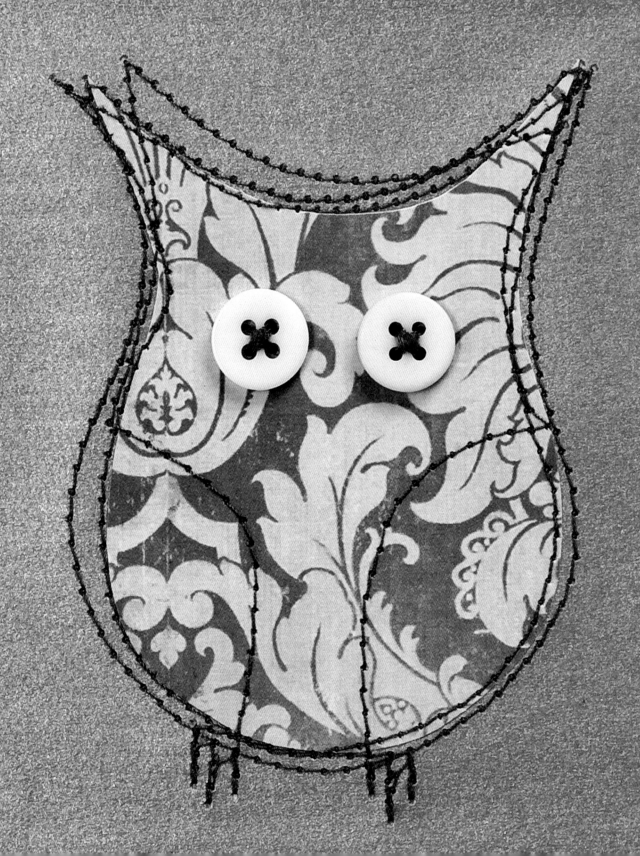

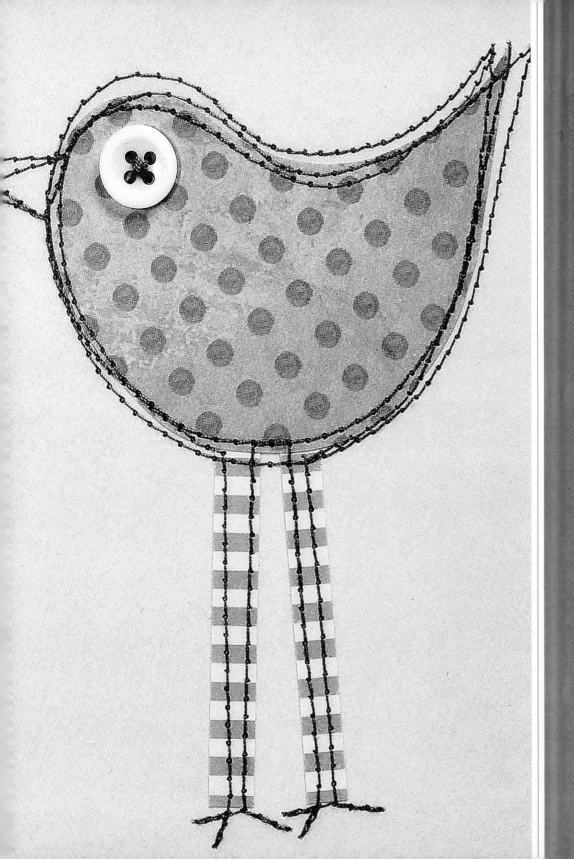

0820 | Tanis Uzwyshyn

0821 | Tanis Uzwyshyn

0822 | Laura McFadden

0823 | Tanis Uzwyshyn

0825-0827 | Carolynn DeCillo

0828-0829 | Heather Price

0831 | Andrea McFadden

0832 | Hilary Pfeifer for Constance Kay

0833 | Carol Greaves

0834 | Jannie Ho

0835 | Hilary Pfeifer for Constance Kay

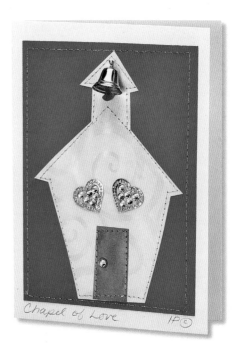

0836 | Hilary Pfeifer for Constance Kay

0837 | Belinda Moon

0838 | Patricia Wilson Nguyen

0839 | Lila Ruby King

0840 | Tanis Uzwyshyn

0841 | Jeanette Imer

0842 | Christina Bevilacqua

0843 | Tanis Uzwyshyn

0844 | Tanis Uzwyshyn

0845 | Tanis Uzwyshyn

0846 | Amy Rowan

0847 | Janet Taylor Pickett

0848 | Janet Taylor Pickett

0849 | Janet Taylor Pickett

0850 | melissahead designs

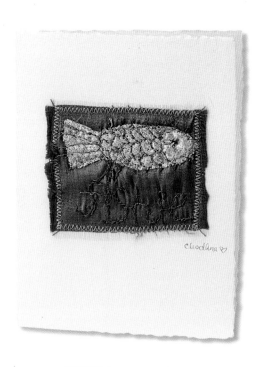

0851 | Cliodhna Quinlan

0852 | Ann Martin

0853 | Belinda Moon

0854 | Marcia Hermann, Julia Anderson & Liza A

0855 | Tanis Uzwyshyn

0856 | Etheland Iris

0857 | Marcia Hermann, Julia Anderson & Liza A

0858 | Ann Martin

0859 | Belinda Moon

0860 | Marcia Hermann, Julia Anderson & Liza A

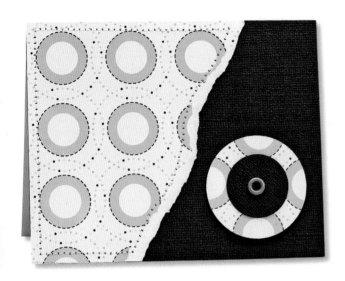

0863 | melissahead designs

0864 | melissahead designs

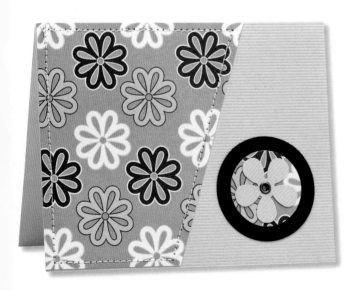

0865 | melissahead designs

0866 | melissahead designs

0867 | Cliodhna Quinlan

0868 | Kelly M. King

Happy Birthday

0869 | Alicia Holland

0870 | Cliodhna Quinlan

0871 | Ellen Wineberg

0872 | Sooziebee

0873 | Ellen Wineberg

thank you

0874 | Tori Rieger

0875 | Susan Delsandro Hellier

0876-0877 | Sooziebee

COLLECTIVE ATTITUDE   225/350   THOMAS COX 12-92

0878 | Thomas Cox

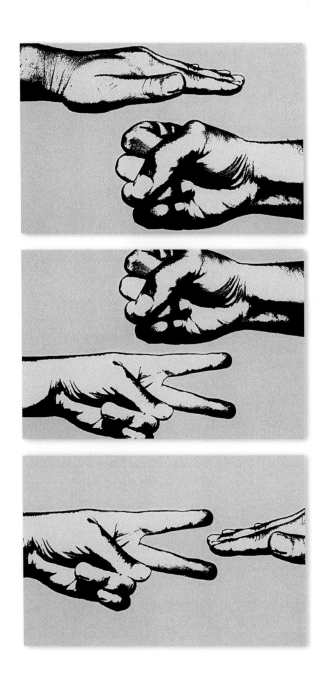

0879-0881 | Alisha Gould Designs

0882 | Carolynn DeCillo

0883 | Machi Ue

0884 | Machi Ue

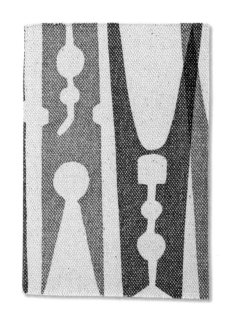

0885 | Machi Ue

0886 | Hilary Pfeifer for Constance Kay

0887 | Amy Stocklein

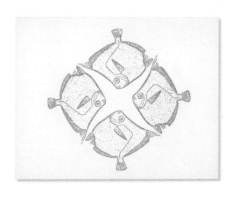

0888 | Sub-Studio

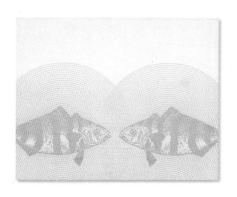

0889 | Sub-Studio

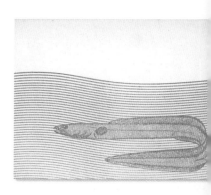

0890 | Sub-Studio

0891 | Sub-Studio

0892 | Sub-Studio

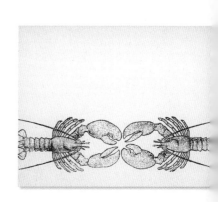

0893 | Sub-Studio

0894 | Sub-Studio

0895 | Sub-Studio

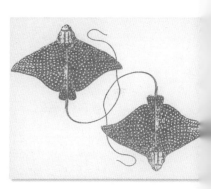

0896 | Sub-Studio

0898 | Laura McFadden

0899 | Carol Greaves

0900 | Machi Ue

0901 | Laura McFadden

0902 | Maggie French

0903 | Sub-Studio

0904 | Pinecone + Chickadee

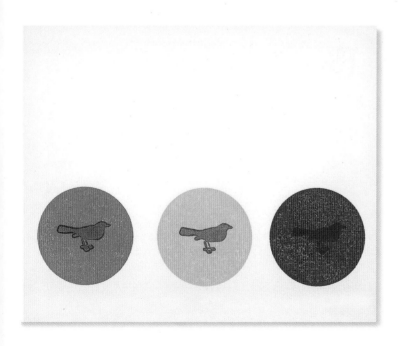

0905 | Megan Dortch for Empty George

0906 | Beau Ideal Editions

0907 | Karena Colquhoun

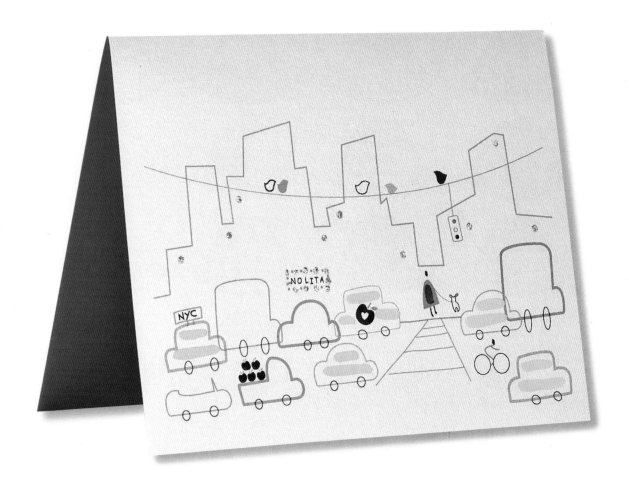

0908 | Loi Luc

0909 | Loi Luc

0910 | guavah designs

0911 | guavah designs

0912 | Loi Luc

0913 | Loi Luc

0914 | guavah designs

0915 | Loi Luc

0916 | guavah designs

0917 | guavah designs

0918 | Betsy Wilson

0919 | Betsy Wilson

0920 | Betsy Wilson

0921 | Hadley Hutton

0922 | ohSmile by eva

0923 | Beau Ideal Editions

0924 | ohSmile by eva

0925 | ohSmile by eva

0926 | Beau Ideal Editions

0927 | ohSmile by eva

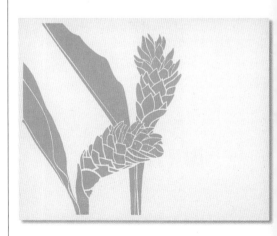

0928 | Sub-Studio

0929 | Michelle Kim

0930 | Michelle Kim

0931 | Michelle Kim

0932 | Meri Meri Inc

0933 | Angela Liguori

0934 | Loi Luc

0935 | Trina Lucido for Constance Kay

0936 | Loi Luc

0937 | Loi Luc

0938 | Susan Gujral for Constance Kay

0989 | Loi Luc

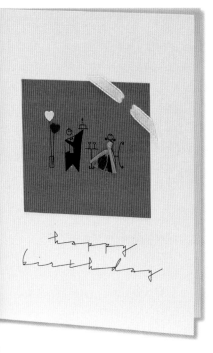

0940 | Loi Luc

0941 | Loi Luc

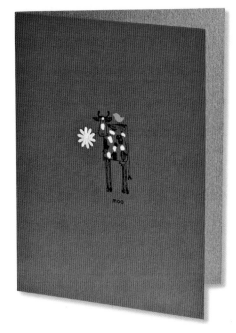

0942 | Loi Luc

0943 | Loi Luc

0944 | Loi Luc

0945 | Julie Steinhilber

0946 | Beau Ideal Editions

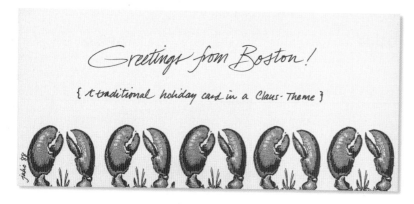

0947 | Julie Steinhilber

0948 | Angela Liguori

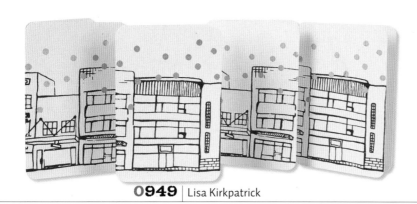

0949 | Lisa Kirkpatrick

0950 | Angela Liguori

0951 | Laura McFadden

0952-0953 | Jenn Mason

0954 | Joel C. Adamich

Women do not live by bread alone...

0955 | Laura Taylor Mark

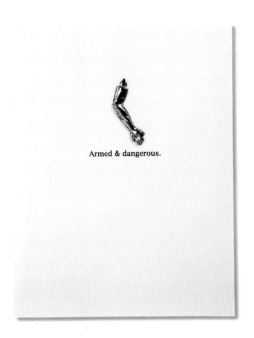

Armed & dangerous.

0956 | Alicia Holland

Break a leg.

0957 | Alicia Holland

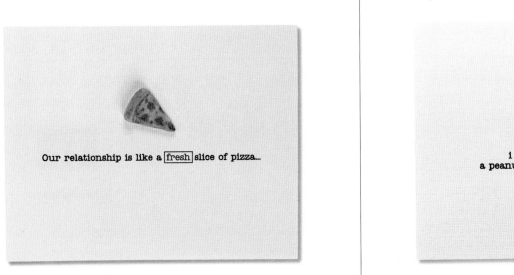

Our relationship is like a [fresh] slice of pizza...

0958 | Laura Taylor Mark

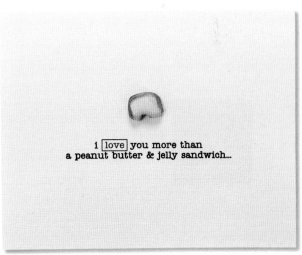

i [love] you more than
a peanut butter & jelly sandwich...

0959 | Laura Taylor Mark

0960 | sonya jf barnett, stüsh

0961 | sonya jf barnett, stüsh

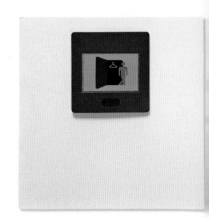

0962 | sonya jf barnett, stüsh

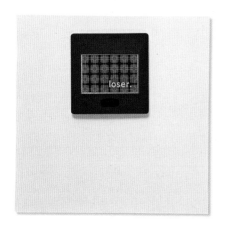

0963 | sonya jf barnett, stüsh

0964 | sonya jf barnett, stüsh

0965 | sonya jf barnett, stüsh

0966 | sonya jf barnett, stüsh

0967 | sonya jf barnett, stüsh

0968 | sonya jf barnett, stüsh

0969 | sonya jf barnett, stüsh

0970 | Amy Rowan

0971 | Christina Riber

0972 | Anne Cresci

0973 | Patricia Wilson Nguyen

0974 | Amy Stocklein

0975 | Patricia Wilson Nguyen

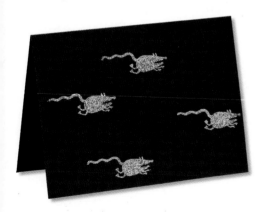

0976 | Keri Straus

0977 | Julie Steinhilber

0978 | Allyson Nickowitz Ross

0979 | Amy Rowan

0980 | Laura McFadden

0981 | Anna Herrick

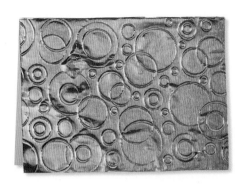

0982 | Anna Herrick

0983 | Anna Herrick

0984 | Raimbow Tree

0985 | Anna Herrick

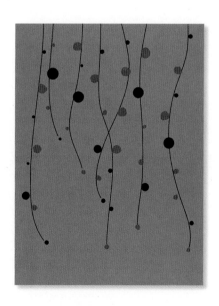

0986 | Loi Luc

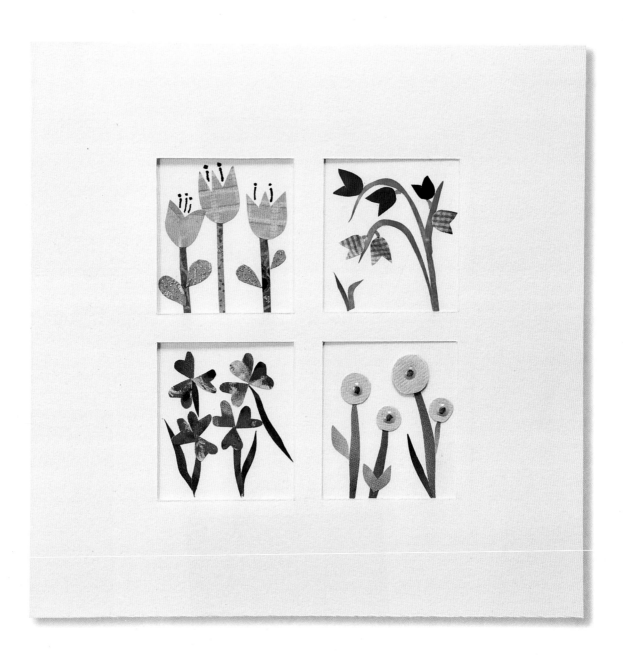

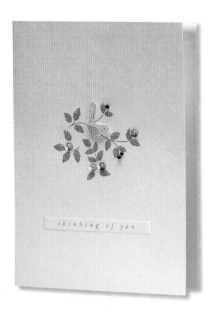

0988 | Meri Meri Inc

0990 | Laura McFadden

0989 | Anna Herrick

0991 | Loi Luc

0992 | Megan Dortch for Empty George

0993 | Joel C. Adamich

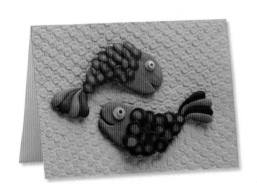

0994 | Anna Herrick

0995 | Jenn Mason

0996 | Angela Liguori

0997 | Charlotte Canup

0998 | Meri Meri Inc

0999 | Betsy Wilson

JOY RIDE   10/250   THOMAS COX 12·2005

1000 | Thomas Cox

ARTIST INDEX

RESOURCES

A.C. Moore
www.acmoore.com

Archiver's
www.archiversonline.com

The Art Store
Blick Company
www.artstore.com

CardBlanks
(Canada and US)
www.cardblanks.com

Charmed Cards
& Crafts (UK)
www.charmedcardsand-
crafts.co.uk

Cheddar Stamper (UK)
www.cheddarstamper.co.uk

Crafts, Etc.
www.craftsetc.com

Create for Less
www.createforless.com

Creative Crafts (UK)
www.creativecrafts.co.uk

Curry's Art Store (Canada)
www.currys.com

Dick Blick
www.dickblick.com

Daniel Smith
www.danielsmith.com

Eckersley's Arts, Crafts,
and Imagination
(New South Wales,
Queensland, South Australia,
and Victoria)
www.eckersleys.com.au

Fabric Place
www.fabricplace.com

Graphigro (France)
www.graphigro.com

HobbyCraft Group Limited
(UK)
www.hobbycraft.co.uk

Jo-Ann Fabrics
www.joann.com

John Lewis (UK)
www.johnlewis.co.uk

Kate's Paperie
www.katespaperie.com

Lazar StudioWerx Inc
(Canada)
www.lazarstudiowerx.com

Making Memories
www.makingmemories.com

Memory Villa
www.memoryvilla.com

Michaels, The Arts
& Craft Store
www.michaels.com

OfficeMax
www.officemax.com

Paper Source
www.paper-source.com

Pearl Art and Craft Supply
www.pearlpaint.com

Staples
www.staples.com

Target
www.target.com

T N Lawrence
& Son Ltd (UK)
www.lawrence.co.uk

Vertecchi (Rome, Italy)
www.vertecchi.com

ACKNOWLEDGMENTS

I'd like to thank my co-author, Deborah Baskin, who gave me major support throughout the entire year. With her keen eye and incredible aesthetic sense, she helped me weed through thousands of cards and selected the best. I'd also like to thank my friends, Carolynn DeCillo and Paul DiMattia, who helped out with layout when I needed it most.

I'd like to thank all of the folks at Quarry Books who made this book possible. Mary Ann Hall, the fearless acquisitions editor who has always supported me despite my inexperience. David Martinell, the backbone of the design department, who remained calm and on top of all of the details. Rosalind Wanke, the creative director who steered the layouts in a better direction—thank you! More gratefulness to Betsy Gammons and Cora Hawks who managed all of the photography and production.

ABOUT THE AUTHORS

Laura McFadden is a freelance art director living in Somerville, Massachusetts. She is author of *100 Ideas for Stationery, Cards, and Invitations.* She is co-author, with April Paffrath, of *The Artful Bride* wedding series.

Deborah Baskin is an architect living in Somerville, Massachusetts. She specializes in residential design as well as commercial interior projects.